Sally 1/2

Lehrwerk für den Englischunterricht in Klasse 1/2

Activity Book 1/2

Erarbeitet von
Jasmin Brune
Daniela Elsner
Stefanie Gleixner-Weyrauch
Marion Lugauer
Sabine Schwarz

Auf der Grundlage der Ausgabe von
Jasmin Brune, Daniela Elsner, Barbara Gleich,
Stefanie Gleixner-Weyrauch, Simone Gutwerk,
Marion Lugauer, Sabine Schwarz

Illustriert von
Barbara Jung, Wilfried Poll,
Sven Leberer und Andreas Fischer

Quellenverzeichnis:
25 Fotos: (Kirsche) Fotolia/© Tim UR; (Banane) Fotolia/© Ian 2010; (Apfel) Fotolia/© siraphol; (Orange) Fotolia/© Egor Rodynchenko; (Zitrone) Fotolia/© anitasstudio; (Birne) Fotolia/© Buriy
26 Fotos: Cornelsen / Johann Jilka, Altenstadt
37 Fotos: (ob. li.) Shutterstock/michaeljung; (Mi. li.) Shutterstock/Michal Kowalski; (Mi. re.) Shutterstock/stockyimages; (ob. re.) Shutterstock.com/Roman White
42 Fotos: Cornelsen / Johann Jilka, Altenstadt

Illustrationen:
Andreas Fischer: S. 47, 69
Barbara Jung: Kapitelvignetten, Medien-Sallys, S. 5, 6 (winkende Sally), 7, 8, 9, 14, 16 (Gesichter), 21, 24, 30, 33, 34, 35 (Lineal, Radiergummi, Bleistift, Kleber, Sally), 36 (Kisten), 37 (Silhouette), 39, 40, 41 (Teetassen und -kannen), 43, 44, 48, 49, 50, 51, 54, 55, 58, 59, 60, 63; Beilagen: Amsel, Fische, Spinne, Regenwolke, Story „Happy Birthday"
Sven Leberer: S.64/65, 66/67, 68, 71; Beilagen: Story „Goldilocks", Story „The three little pigs"
Wilfried Poll: Selbsteinschätzungs-Sallys, S. 1, 4, 6, 10, 11, 12, 13, 15, 16, 17, 18, 19, 20, 22, 23, 25, 27, 28, 29, 31, 32, 35 (Buch, Federmäppchen, Ranzen), 36, 38, 41 (Sally-Comic), 45, 46, 47 (Karotte), 50 (Tiere Aufgabe 3), 52/53, 56, 57, 61, 62; Beilagen

Beratende Mitwirkung: Sarah Filiatrault-Forkmann, Ottawa, Kanada (englischsprachige Texte)

Redaktion: Salomé Dick, Berlin
Umschlagkonzept: Corinna Babylon, Berlin
Umschlagillustration: Wilfried Poll
Layout: Ungermeyer: Rosemeyer + Unger GbR
Technische Umsetzung: PER MEDIEN & MARKETING GmbH, Braunschweig

www.cornelsen.de

1. Auflage, 1. Druck 2025

Alle Drucke dieser Auflage sind inhaltlich unverändert und können im Unterricht nebeneinander verwendet werden.

© 2025 Cornelsen Verlag GmbH, Mecklenburgische Str. 53, 14197 Berlin,
E-Mail: service@cornelsen.de

Das Werk und seine Teile sind urheberrechtlich geschützt. Jede Nutzung in anderen als den gesetzlich zugelassenen Fällen bedarf der vorherigen schriftlichen Einwilligung des Verlages. Hinweis zu §§ 60 a, 60 b UrhG: Weder das Werk noch seine Teile dürfen ohne eine solche Einwilligung an Schulen oder in Unterrichts- und Lehrmedien (§ 60 b Abs. 3 UrhG) vervielfältigt, insbesondere kopiert oder eingescannt, verbreitet oder in ein Netzwerk eingestellt oder sonst öffentlich zugänglich gemacht oder wiedergegeben werden. Dies gilt auch für Intranets von Schulen und anderen Bildungseinrichtungen.

Der Anbieter behält sich eine Nutzung der Inhalte für Text- und Data-Mining im Sinne § 44 b UrhG ausdrücklich vor.

Druck: Athesiadruck GmbH, Bozen

ISBN 978-3-464-81435-2

Inhalt

Hello 🟢 4

Colours 🟢 7

Numbers 🟢 10

My schoolbag 🟢 12

Body and feelings 🟢 15

Toys 🟢 18

Checkpoint 1 🟢 21

Animals 🟢 22

Fruit 🟢 25

Clothes 🟢 29

Family 🟢 32

Checkpoint 2 🟢 34

At school 🟣 35

Body and clothes 🟣 38

It's teatime 🟣 41

Checkpoint 3 🟣 43

Hobbies 🟣 44

Vegetables 🟣 46

Weather 🟣 48

Farm animals 🟣 50

Checkpoint 4 🟣 51

Seasons and special days:

Seasons 🟣 52

Happy birthday 🟣 54

Happy Halloween 🟣 56

Merry Christmas 🟢 + 🟣 57

Happy Easter 🟢 + 🟣 60

Show what you know 🟣 63

Fairy tales and stories:

The three little pigs 🟢 64

Goldilocks and the three bears 🟢 / 🟣 66

Enormous Elephant 🟣 68

Minibooks 69

empfohlene Zuordnung:
🟢 Klasse 1
🟣 Klasse 2
🟢 + 🟣 Klasse 1 **und** 2
🟢 / 🟣 Klasse 1 **oder** 2

 Hello

✎ ① **Draw.**

👥 ② **Say your name.**

4 four

Hello

✂ ① **Colour.**

🔊 2 👂 💬 ② **Listen and act out the rhyme.**

 🔊 3

five 5

Hello

🔊 3 👂 👆 ① **Listen and point.**

👂 💬 ② **Listen and tick or number.**

✂️ ③ **Draw.**

 ④ **Sing.**

Sing and record.

6   six   🔊 4

Colours

1 Listen and colour.

 **Colours**

🎧 👆 ① Listen and point.   ✂ ② Colour the flames.

8 eight

Colours

1 Play the game.

Numbers

🎧 ✂️ ① **Listen and colour.**

💬 ② **Tell.**

10 ten

Numbers

🔊 6 👂 ✂ ① **Listen and draw.**

💬 ② Say the rhyme.

 🔊 12

eleven 11

 **My schoolbag**

1 **Listen and draw.**

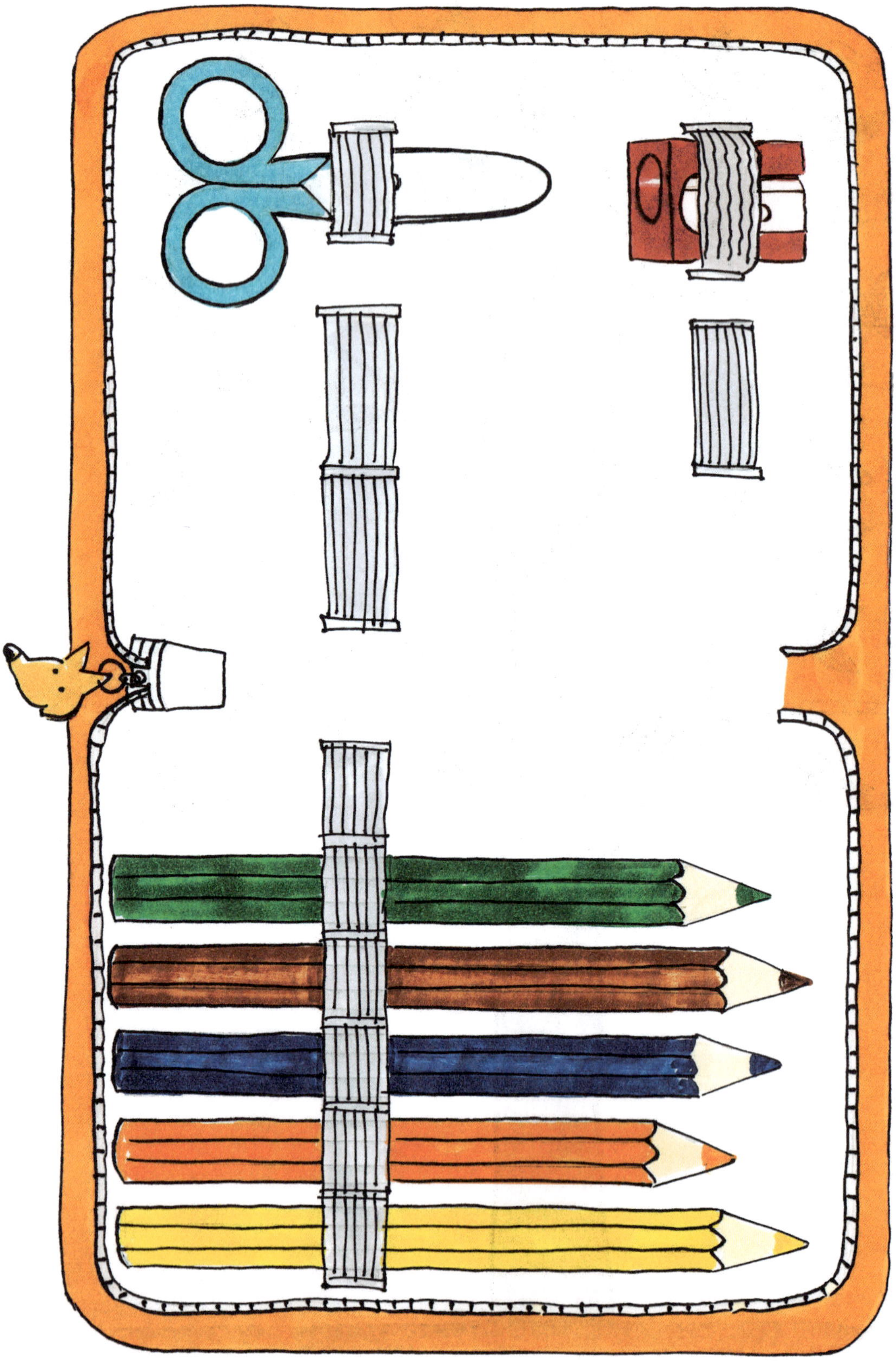

2 **Tell.**

My schoolbag

1 Listen and draw lines.

2 Tell.

  16

thirteen 13

My schoolbag

1. **Circle.**

2. **Tell.**

14 fourteen

Body and feelings

  Draw.

  Tell.

fifteen 15

 **Body and feelings**

🔊 9 👂 ✏️ ① **Listen and draw lines.**

💬 ② **Say the rhyme.**

Body and feelings

- ① Colour.
- ② Count and write. 
- ③ Tell.

seventeen **17**

✂ ① **Colour.**

💬 ② **Tell.**

18 eighteen

Toys

① **Listen and colour.**

② **Draw.**

③ **Tell.**

nineteen **19**

 Toys

| 1 Colour. | 2 Play the game. |

Show what you know

1 **Look and tell.**

twenty-one 21

 **Animals**

🔊 14 👂 ✂️ ① **Listen and colour.**

🎵 ② **Sing.**

Sing and record.

Animals

✏️ ① **Draw a line.**

twenty-three 23

Animals

  1 Stick in and colour.   💬 **2** Tell.

24 twenty-four

Fruit

1. Draw lines.
2. Colour.

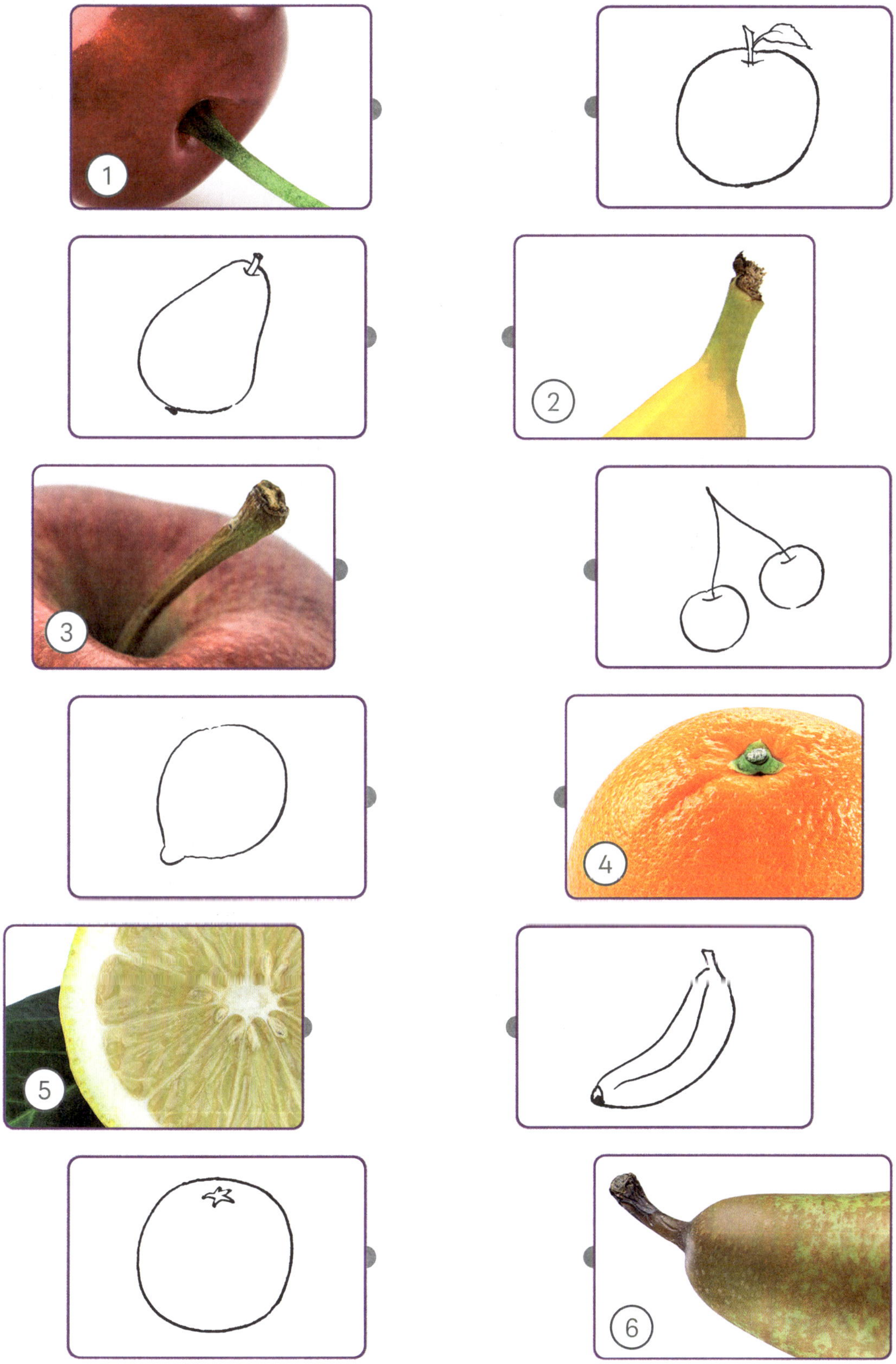

 **Fruit**

1 **Listen and number.**

2 Let's make a banana milk shake.

Fruit

1 **Count and write.**

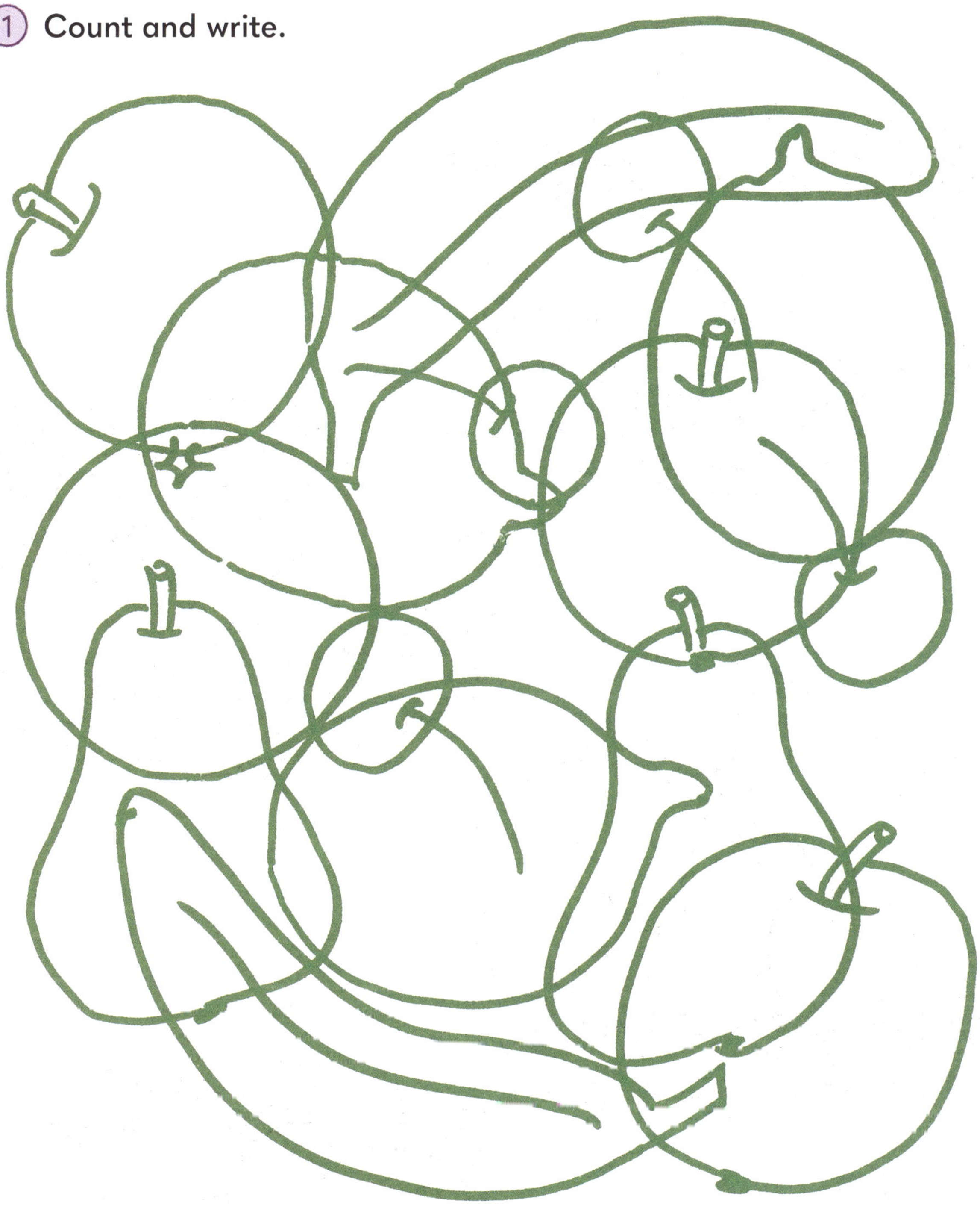

2 **Tell.**

twenty-seven 27

 Fruit

1 **Listen and number.**

2 **Tell.**

Clothes

1 Listen and stick in.   2 Tell.

 34

twenty-nine 29

 Clothes

1 Listen and draw lines.

2 Tell.

3 Colour and tell.

Clothes

 ① Draw your perfect outfit. Present.

  Family

✏️ ① **Circle.**

💬 ② **Tell.**

Family

1 **Draw or stick in.**

2 **Tell.**

thirty-three 33

 **Show what you know**

💬 1 **Look and tell.**

At school

👂 ✂️ ① Listen and colour.

✏️ ② Write.

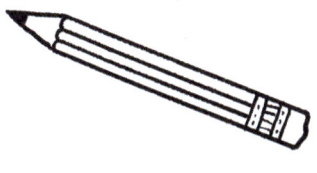
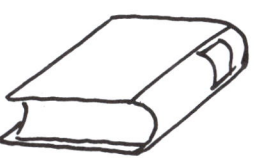

schoolbag

book

pencil

pencil case

rubber

ruler
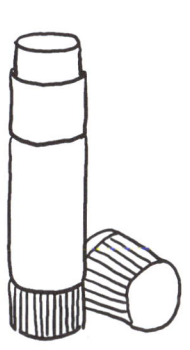

glue stick

 **At school**

1 **Listen and circle.**

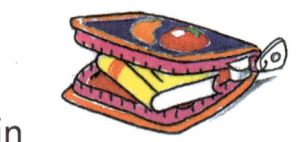 in

 under

 on

 on

 in

 under

 in

 under

 on

2 **Write.**

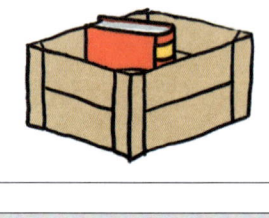

At school

1 Listen and number.

2 Create your dream school uniform. Present.
My school uniform is a ... and a ...

thirty-seven 37

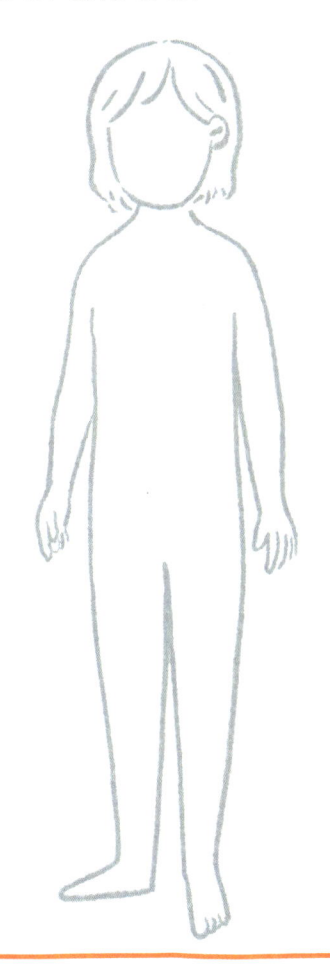

Body and clothes

🔊 19 👂 ✏️ **1** Listen and stick in.

① ② ③ ④ ⑤ ⑥

👂 ✏️ **2** Listen and write.

arms　　feet　　mouth　　eyes
hands　　legs　　nose　　ears

✂️ **3** Colour.

38　thirty-eight　　🔊 45

Body and clothes

1 Listen and number.

2 Colour.

3 Tell.

47

thirty-nine 39

Body and clothes

1 Look, tell and write.

shoes   T-shirt   skirt   trousers

40 forty

It's teatime

1 Listen and draw.

2 Colour and tell.

48

forty-one 41

It's teatime

1 Listen and number.

2 Let's have a tea party.

42 forty-two 51

Show what you know

1 Look and tell.

forty-three 43

Hobbies

1 **Colour and write.**

ball   tablet   stickers
playing cards   inline skates

2 **Tell.**

Hobbies

1 What's missing? Tell.   2 Draw.

forty-five 45

Vegetables

1. Stick in.

2. Tell.

3. Draw lines and write.

lettuce   carrot   bean

radish   cucumber   tomato

46   forty-six

Vegetables

1. Listen and number.

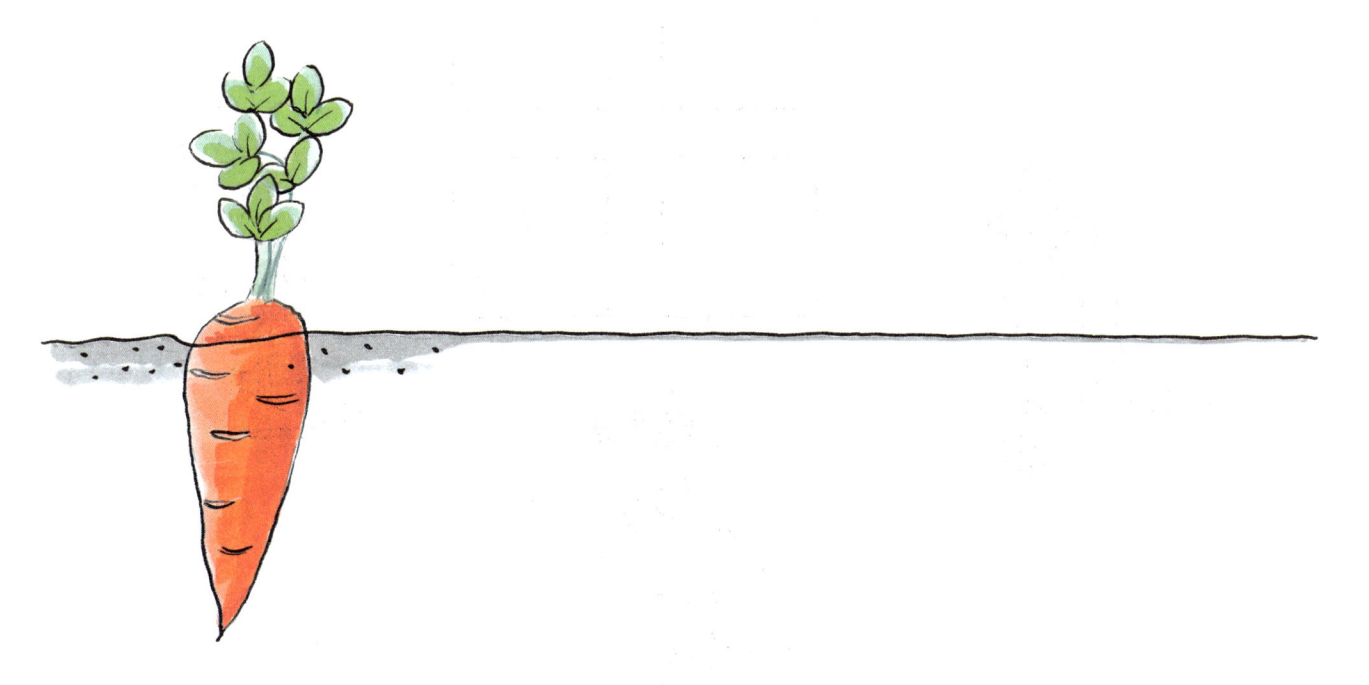

2. Read and write.

Come and help us!

3. Stick in and draw.

4. Tell.

55

forty-seven 47

Weather

1. Read and write.

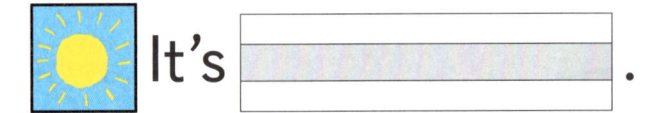

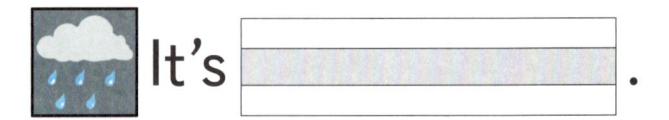

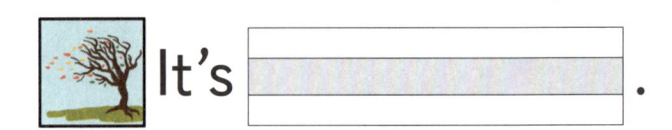

It's _____.   It's _____.

It's _____.   It's _____.

rainy   windy   sunny   snowy

2. Listen and number.

3. Draw lines.

4. Tell.

Weather

🔊 23 👂 ✂️ ① **Listen and stick in.**

🦘 ② **Act out the rhyme.**

🔊 60

forty-nine 49

Farm animals

👆 ① Point and count.

👂 ✏️ ② Listen and number.

✏️ ③ Write.

pig   hen   goose   duck

horse    cow    sheep

50 fifty 🔊 63

Show what you know

1 Look and tell.

fifty-one 51

Seasons

1. Listen and point.
2. Colour and draw.

It's autumn.

It's winter.

Seasons

3 Write.

It's spring.

It's summer.

fifty-three 53

Happy birthday

1. Count and write.

2. Colour and write.

3. Tell.

4. Write.

blue   balloon   orange   present   brown
cake   red   candle   green   party hat

54   fifty-four

Happy birthday

1 Listen and stick in.

2 Act out the story.

Make a video.

74

fifty-five 55

Happy Halloween

1 Circle.   2 Colour and write.

Happy Halloween!

56 fifty-six

Merry Christmas

1. Listen and point.

2. Colour.

3. Tell.

fifty-seven 57

Merry Christmas

1 Make your own wish list. Draw or stick in. Present.

58　fifty-eight

Merry Christmas

1 Listen and draw. 2 Write.

Merry Christmas!

3 Tell.

81 fifty-nine 59

Happy Easter

1 **Listen and colour.**

2 **Tell.**

sixty

Happy Easter

1 **Listen and draw.**

sixty-one 61

Happy Easter

1 **Colour.**

2 **Tell.**

62 sixty-two

Show what you know

1 Play the game in your group.

sixty-three **63**

The three little pigs

1 Listen and stick in.

The three little pigs

2 Act out the story.

sixty-five 65

Goldilocks and the three bears

1. Listen and point.

2. Listen and colour.

Goldilocks and the three bears

3 Act out the story.

Make a video.

sixty-seven 67

Enormous Elephant

👂 👉 ① Listen and point.

👂 ✏️ ② Listen, read and stick in.

68 sixty-eight 🔊 92

Sally 1/2 – Activity Book © 2025 Cornelsen Verlag GmbH, Berlin.
Alle Rechte vorbehalten. Illustrationen: Andreas Fischer

Sally 1/2 – Activity Book © 2025 Cornelsen Verlag GmbH, Berlin.
Alle Rechte vorbehalten. Illustrationen: Sven Leberer

Sally 1/2 Activity Book © 2025 Cornelsen Verlag GmbH, Berlin.

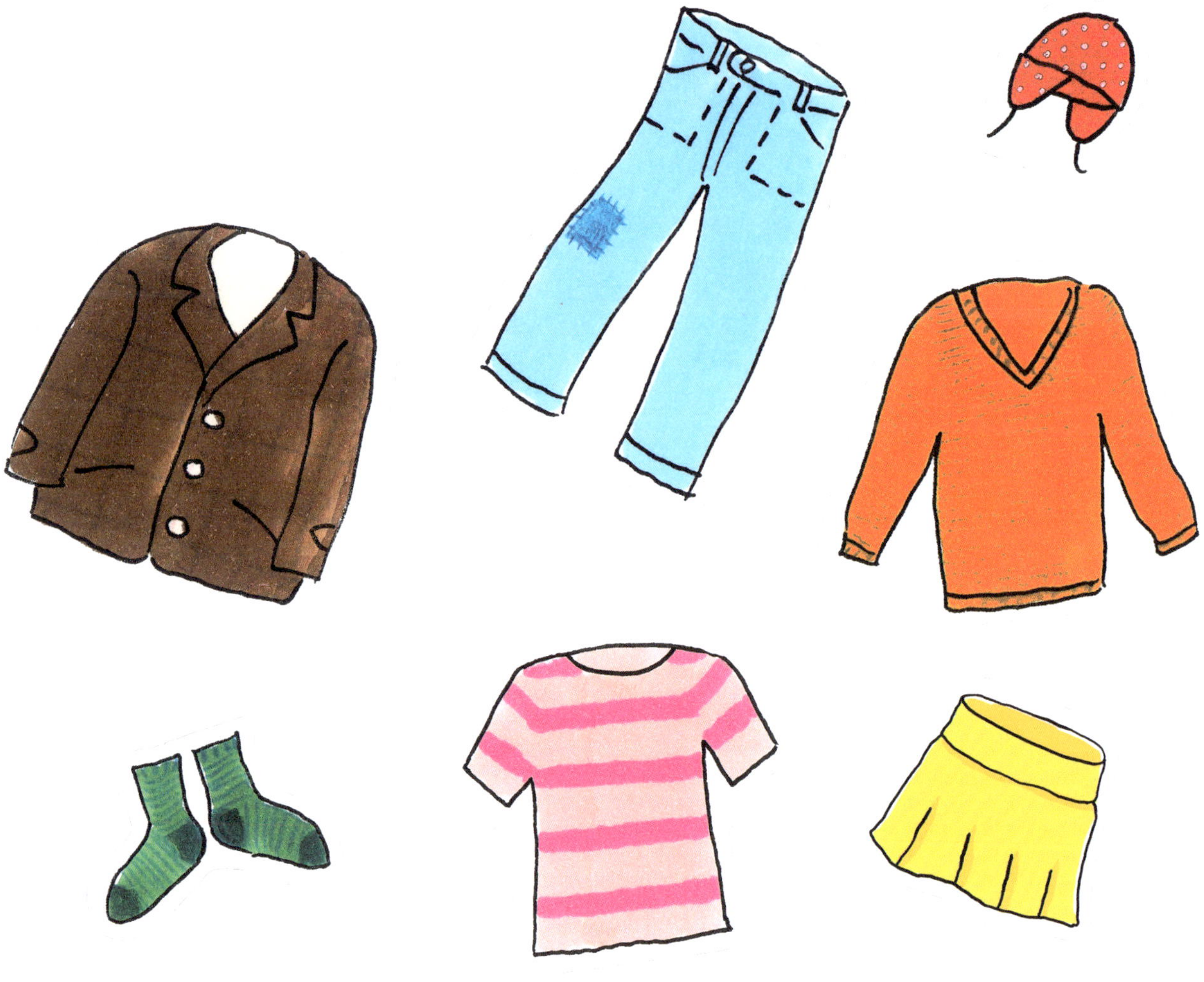

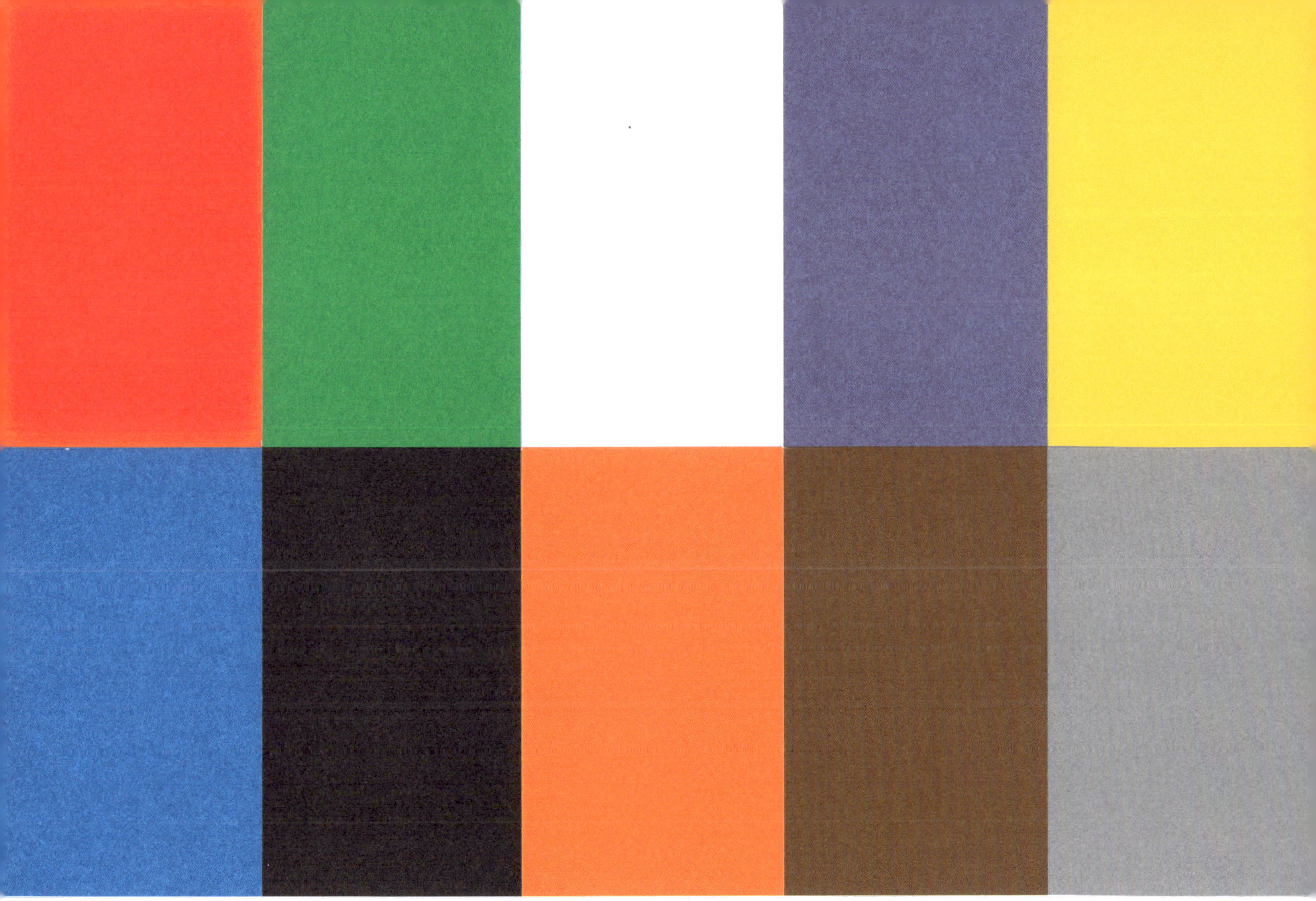

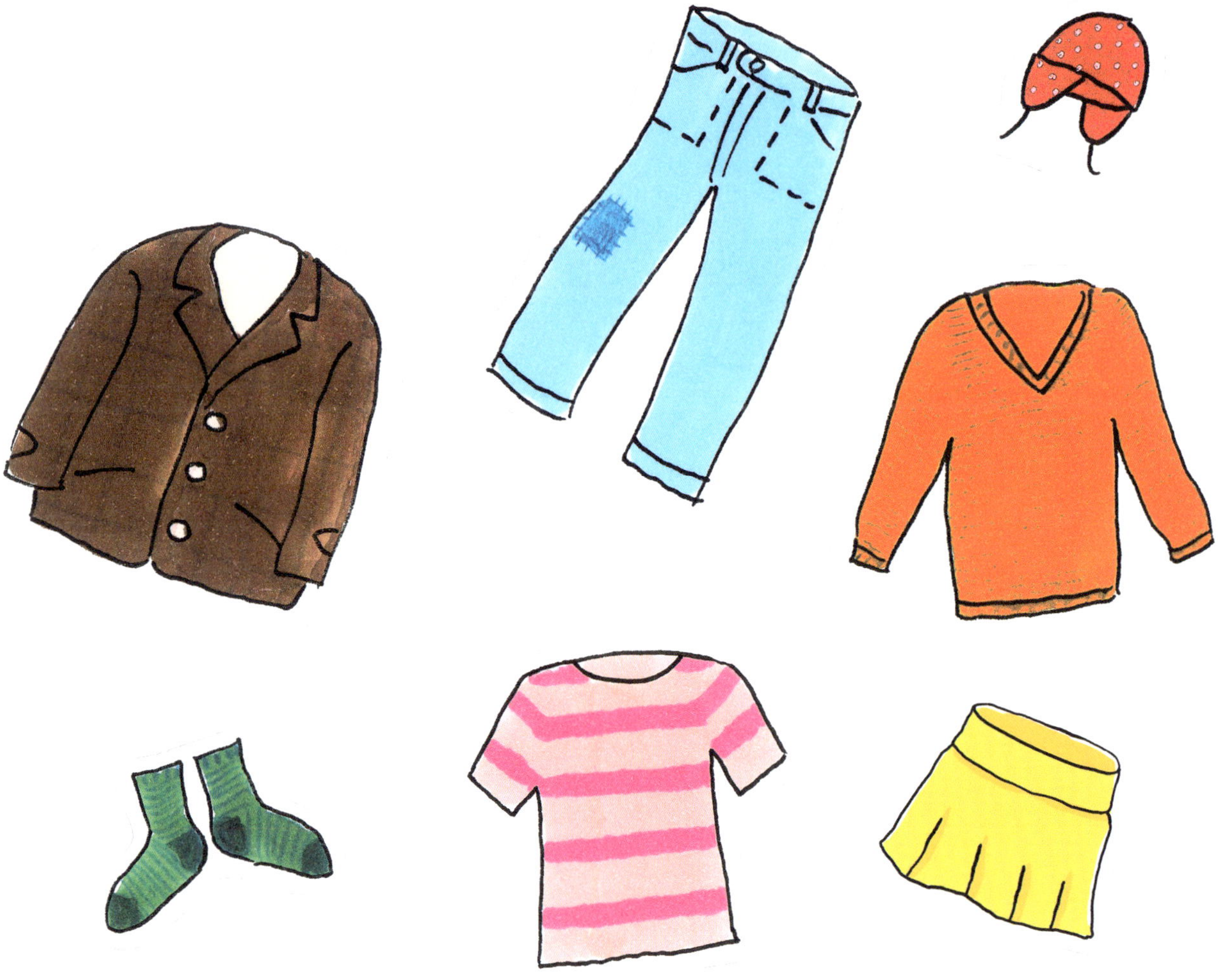

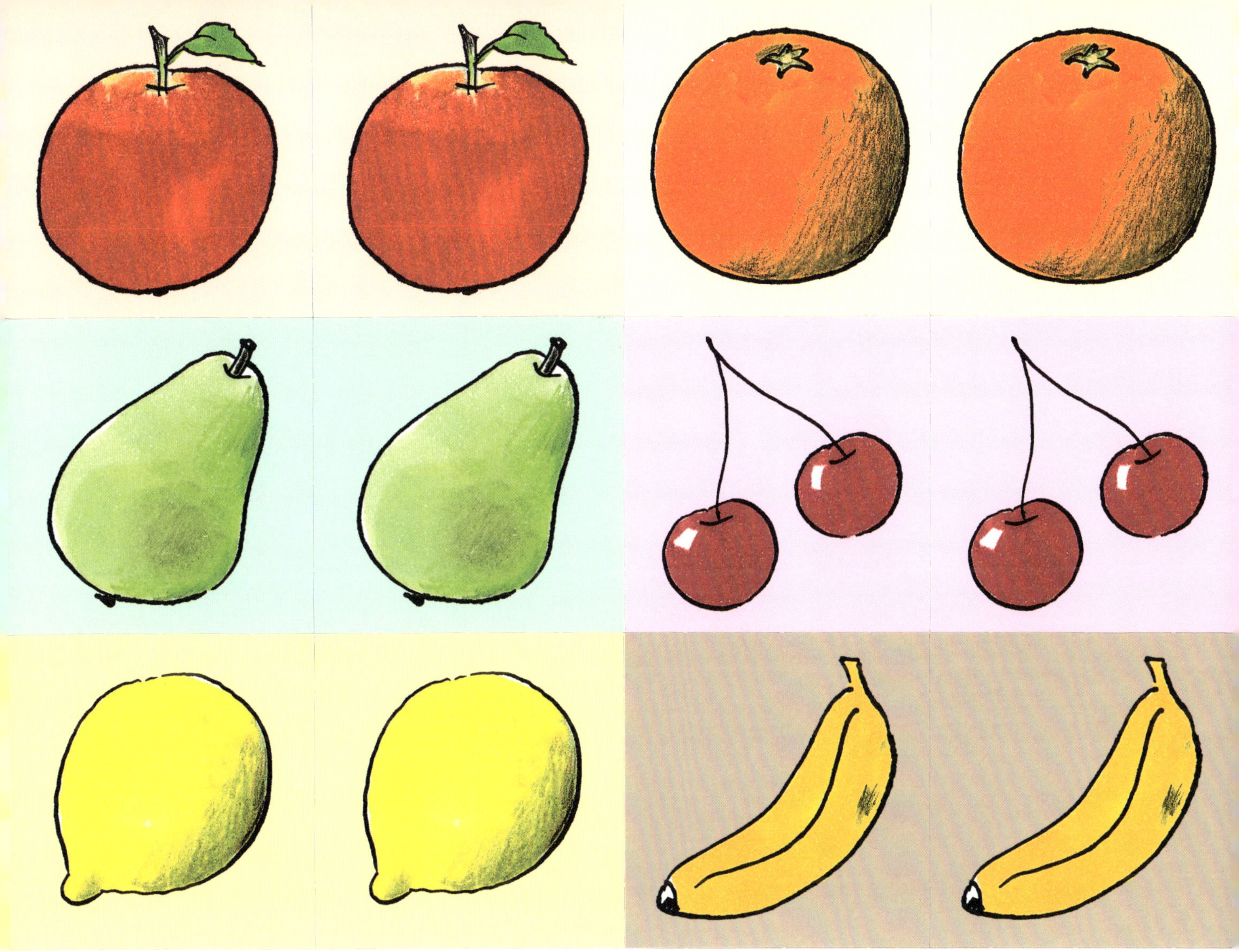

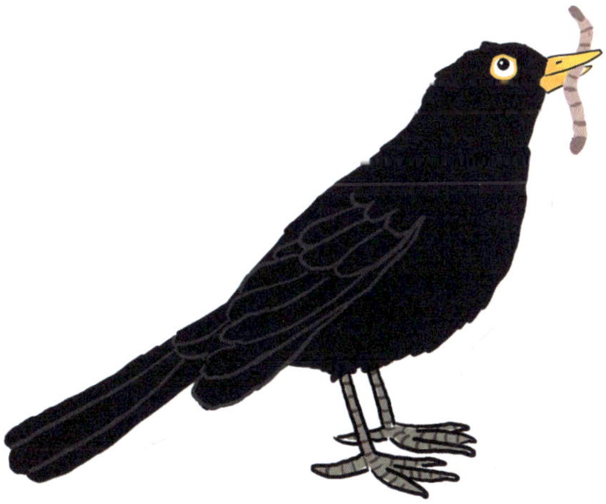

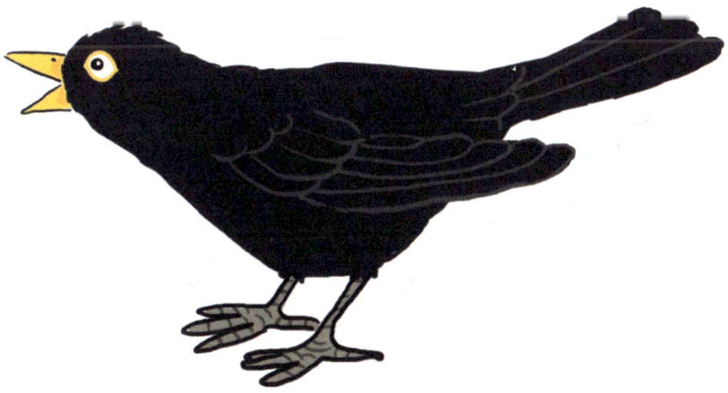

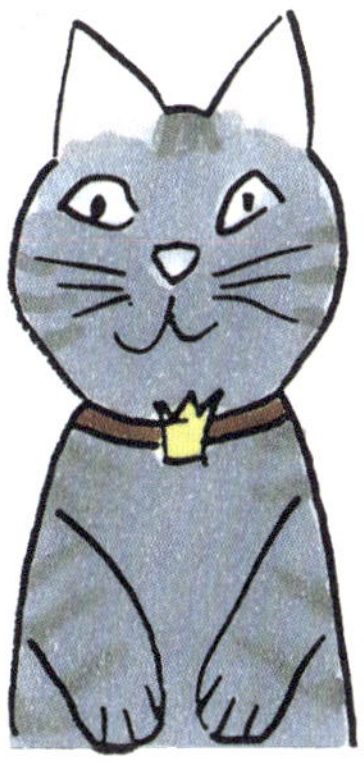
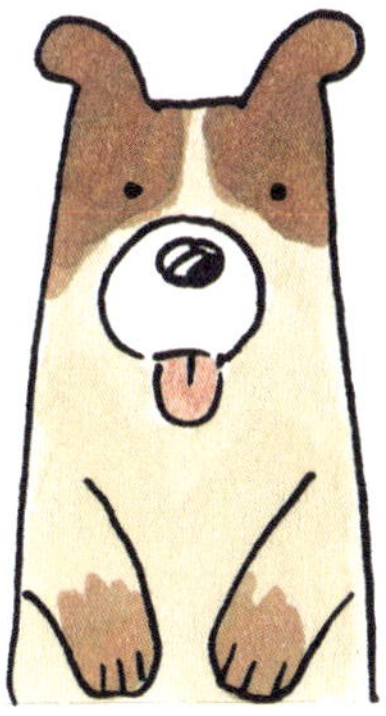
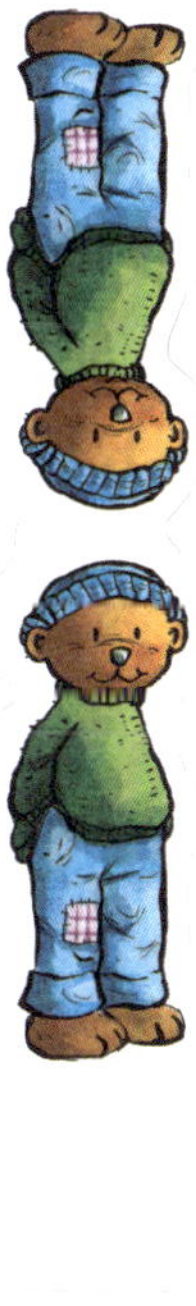
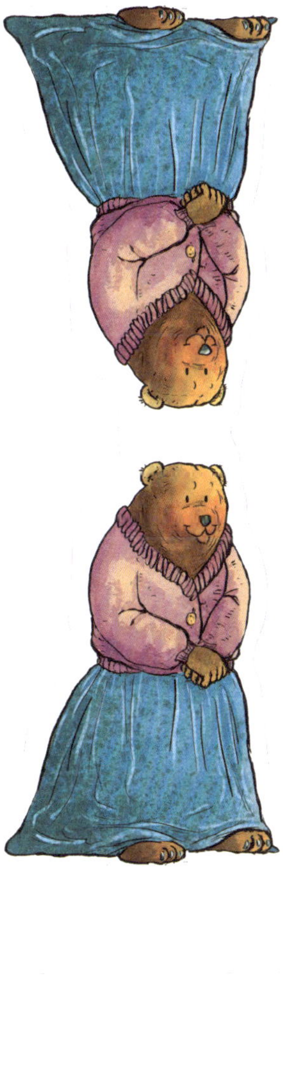
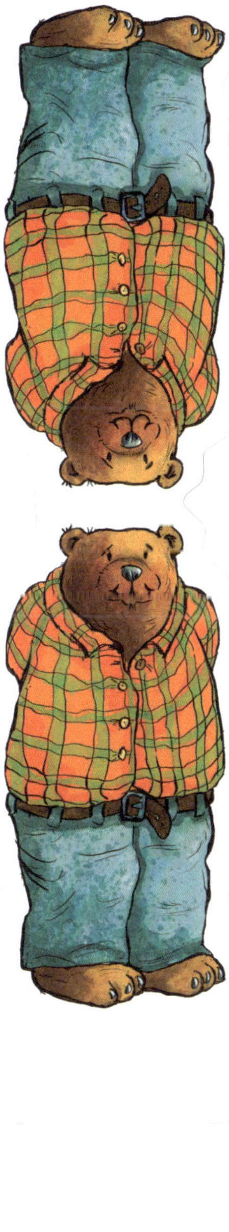
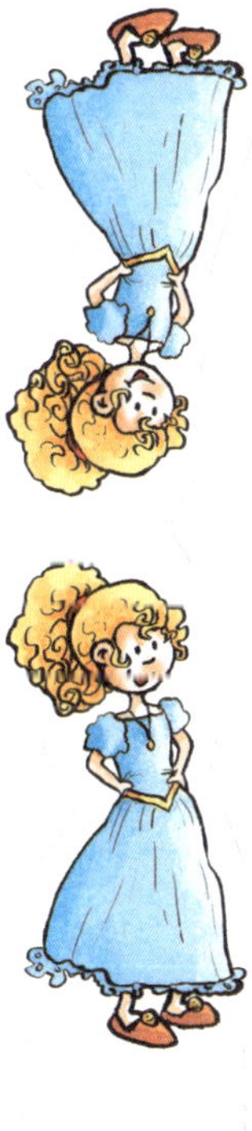

Sally 1/2 Activity Book © 2025 Cornelsen Verlag GmbH, Berlin.

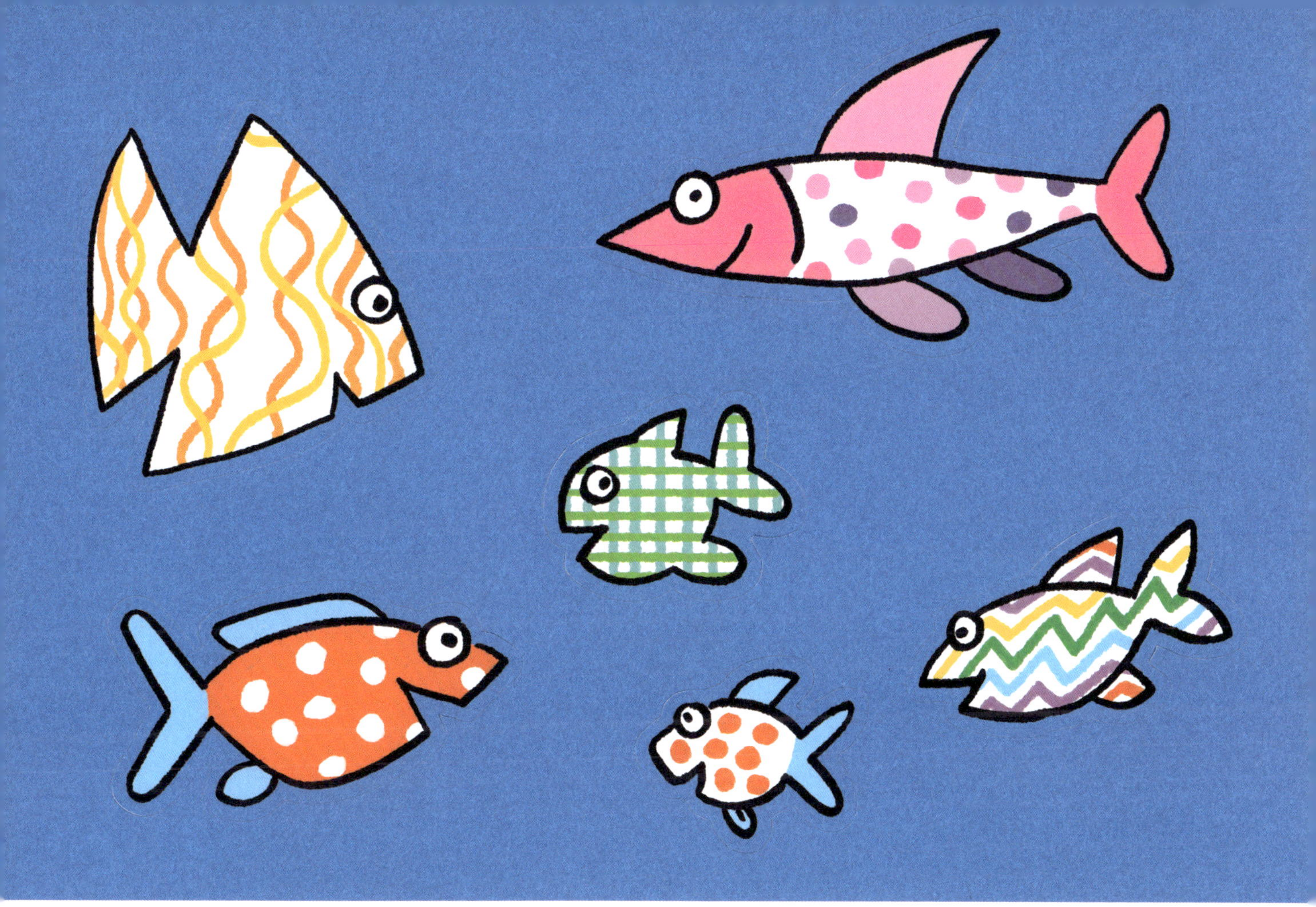

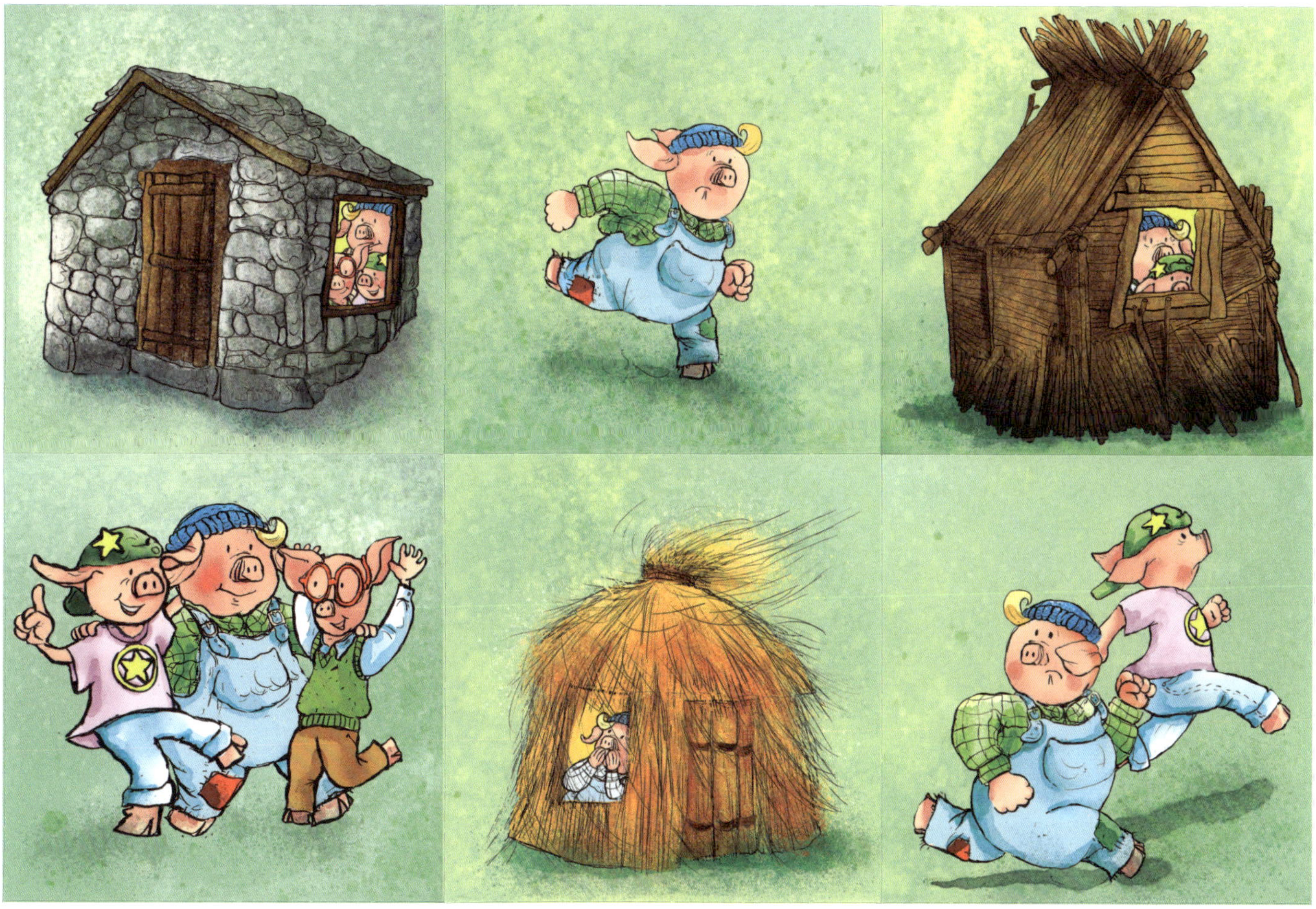

Sally 1/2 Activity Book © 2025 Cornelsen Verlag GmbH, Berlin.

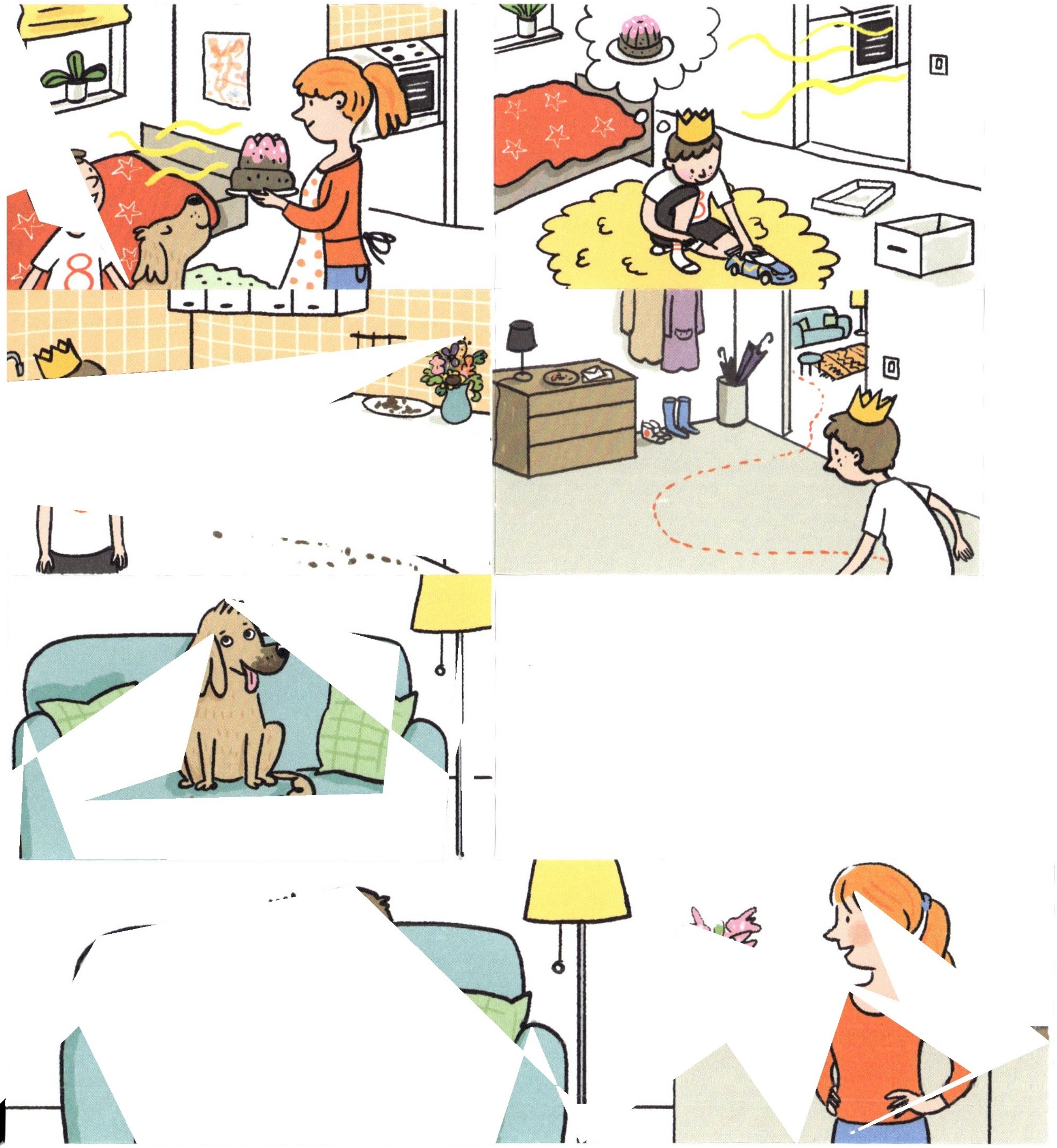

Hello!
How are you?   I'm bored.   Let's go to
                            New York!

Hello!
How are you?   I'm bored.   Let's go to
                            New York!